NCLUSION
Pocketbook

By Niki Elliot,
Elaine Doxey and
Val Stephenson

Published by:

Teachers' Pocketbooks
Laurel House, Station Approach,
Alresford, Hampshire SO24 9JH, UK
Tel: +44 (0)1962 735573
Fax: +44 (0)1962 733637
E-mail: sales@teacherspocketbooks.co.uk
Website: www.teacherspocketbooks.co.uk

*Teachers' Pocketbooks is an imprint of
Management Pocketbooks Ltd.*

With thanks to Brin Best for his help in
launching the series.

All rights reserved. No part of this publication
may be reproduced, stored in a retrieval
system or transmitted in any form, or by any
means, electronic, mechanical, photocopying,
recording or otherwise, without the prior
permission of the publishers.

© Niki Elliot, Elaine Doxey and
    Val Stephenson 2004.

This edition published 2004.
Reprinted, 2006, 2009.

ISBN 978 1903776 58 2

British Library Cataloguing-in-Publication
Data – A catalogue record for this book is
available from the British Library.

Design, typesetting and graphics by Efex Ltd.
Printed in UK.

2   Inclusion

Contents

		Page
 Inclusion is...	Inclusion confusion, what is inclusion?, historical context, factors influencing education policy, how inclusive is the English education system?, what inclusion means for a school and whether it is always right to include, a working definition	9
Building an Inclusive Ethos	Bringing everyone on board, personal beliefs and vision, building learning communities, interpreting the context for your school – using a continuum and SWOT analysis, managing the dilemmas	21
Formulating an Inclusion Policy	The inclusion raft; structuring your policy – vision, principles, aims, practice; monitoring and evaluating	39
Managing Inclusion	The staff team, setting up management structures and allocating responsibilities, time to talk	51
Inclusive Classrooms – Planning & Teaching	The inclusion jigsaw, analysing needs, assessment, setting suitable learning challenges, responding to pupils' needs, access, provision, time to reflect	61
Inclusive Learning Environments	Classroom management, creating calm classrooms, end of lesson or activity, analysis of systems, groupings, peer support strategies, teaching assistants, teamwork, reflection	79
Evaluating Inclusion	How do we know if we're inclusive?; sources of information – students, parents, community, staff; gathering information; analysing hard data; value added; planning for change; what next?; conclusion	95
Further Information	Rights, legislation and guidance, bibliography	115

Introduction

Welcome to The Inclusion Pocketbook.

Why is inclusion so important? Because we all want to feel included!

Feeling left out, inadequate, not wanted, not fitting in, are common human experiences. We all know how they make us feel and we have all seen them happen to other people. This book is about tackling these issues by creating inclusive culture, policy and practice in your school.

It is how society responds to difference that makes some groups of people more vulnerable than others: people with disability, people who find learning very hard or very easy, people from different cultural or language backgrounds, people who face social, emotional or communication difficulties.

Introduction

When you think about each of these groups we all belong to them or have the potential to do so. What happens if you move to another country or even a different bit of this country, if you break a leg, if you have difficulty implementing a new teaching strategy, if your personal circumstances leave you unable to concentrate and short tempered? These challenges may be less severe or shorter term in their effect but they make a point. These 'vulnerable groups' are not 'others', they are us.

Inclusion is about everyone, so the best inclusive practice involves people, plans for difference, anticipates need, picks up quickly when someone is not joining in, or doing as well as they could and takes action.

Introduction

This book is for anyone who has a role in leading and managing inclusion. We aim to provide you with a range of tools, prompts and ideas that will help you establish firm foundations for inclusive practice.

The idea of inclusion can make staff feel anxious about their knowledge and skills and whether or not they are equipped to meet a particular pupil's needs. This is not a book about specialist skills, it is about creating a school in which the majority of additional needs are met by good planning and teaching. A school where staff are able to identify when specialist help and resources are needed without feeling inadequate or uncomfortable about requesting them.

Introduction

The book is structured around four building blocks:

Culture: Beliefs and understanding about inclusion and how these become part of a school's vision and ethos – chapters 1 and 2

Policy: How to describe and let people know what is expected and accepted practice – chapter 3

Practice: How management and classroom practice contribute to inclusion – chapters 4-6

Impact: How to evaluate effectiveness – chapter 7

We have had the pleasure of working with many schools which have been striving to become more inclusive over the years. Our book brings together ideas, attitudes and practice that have contributed to the success of these schools and will do the same for yours.

'Every child has unique characteristics, interests, abilities and learning needs...Education systems should be designed and educational programmes implemented to take into account the wide diversity of these characteristics and needs.'

The Salamanca Statement (UNESCO, 1994)

Inclusion is...

 Building an Inclusive Ethos

 Formulating an Inclusion Policy

 Managing Inclusion

 Inclusive Classrooms – Planning & Teaching

 Inclusive Learning Environments

 Evaluating Inclusion

 Further Information

Inclusion is...

Inclusion confusion!

Inclusion confusion!

What is inclusion?

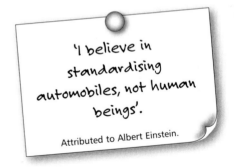

Inclusion isn't:
- Knocking square pegs into round holes
- Making people conform
- About everyone having the same experience
- An afterthought

Inclusion is:
- Celebrating individuality
- Valuing the contributions and views of others
- About valuing your own and other people's cultures
- Providing flexible learning experiences
- Fundamental to good education

'I believe in standardising automobiles, not human beings'.

Attributed to Albert Einstein.

What is inclusion?

Inclusion isn't:
- Another 'apple pie and motherhood' nice idea
- Just about pupils with special educational needs
- Policies and pieces of paper
- Planning lots of individual programmes

Inclusion is:
- Being reflective about practice
- Understanding the context of your school
- Knowing the needs of your pupils
- Changing the organisation of the school to suit the pupils
- About the needs of the whole school community
- Everyone's responsibility

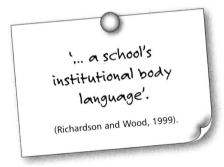

'... a school's institutional body language'.

(Richardson and Wood, 1999).

Factors influencing education policy

The government is signatory to both the Salamanca Statement on inclusive schooling and to the UN Convention on the Rights of the Child: these, along with economic and social issues, have contributed to both legislation and curriculum changes since the 1990s.

The UN Rights of the Child – preparing children for life in a free society.	**Salamanca Statement – recognising and responding to diverse needs.**
Consequences of educational disadvantage on health, poverty and employment.	**The economy – a skilled, flexible and confident workforce.**

Inclusive schools are seen as important factors in developing a cohesive and fair society and in supporting economic prosperity. These are huge challenges.

So how inclusive is the education system in England?

Inclusion now has an established place on the national educational agenda.

The Ofsted framework for inspecting schools places inclusion at its heart:
'An educationally inclusive school is one in which the teaching and learning, achievements, attitudes and well-being of every young person matter.'
(Ofsted 2000)

In 2001 the National Curriculum was extended by the QCA to include pupils of all abilities with the publication of *Planning, Teaching and Assessing the Curriculum for Pupils with Learning Difficulties* containing curriculum and assessment advice for all subjects.

So how inclusive is the education system in England?

The National Curriculum requires schools and teachers to address three key inclusive principles:

1. Setting suitable learning challenges.
2. Responding to pupils' diverse learning needs.
3. Overcoming barriers to learning and assessment for individuals and groups of students.

Every Child Matters extends our thinking and our responsibilities for all children. It challenges us to pursue five outcomes for them:

What does inclusion mean for a school?

- Inclusion is a process, not an endpoint. No individual or organisation can claim to be fully inclusive
- It is, rather, a constant cycle of reflection and adjustment to make your school or classroom more inclusive
- It is about pushing out the boundaries of curriculum design and classroom management, to encompass an ever wider range of students

This is not just a challenge to our planning, it is a challenge to our thinking about familiar systems and structures which we might be comfortable with but which cause others to feel uncomfortable, or excluded.

'The more inclusive a setting, the more it is challenged by diversity and difference.'

(K. Ballard, 1999).

What does inclusion mean for a child?

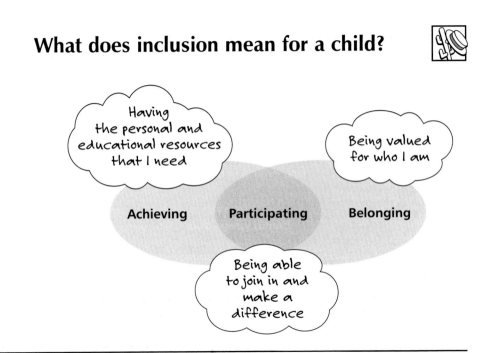

Having the personal and educational resources that I need

Being valued for who I am

Achieving   **Participating**   **Belonging**

Being able to join in and make a difference

Working in partnership to achieve inclusion

Partnership is about:

- Sharing information and ideas
- Changing your mind
- Finding new ways of doing things
- Understanding someone else's perspective
- Pooling resources
- Listening

Partnership can be with:

families   children

health professionals   social care   the voluntary sector

youth services   community workers   police

In partnership we can help families to keep children safe, healthy and able to get the best from being in your school.

A working definition

By drawing together the key features of inclusion from a range of perspectives, we offer this as a starting point from which you can build your own definition of inclusion, one that will have meaning for your school.

Inclusion is a process through which a school's staff:

- Identify the extent to which all children are able to participate in school life, to achieve in line with their potential and to express their individuality
- Analyse and reflect upon their findings
- Collaborate to create the conditions that promote increased participation and achievement, and develop individuality

'An inclusive school recognises and respects the cultural and personal identities and life-experiences of its pupils or students, and helps them to develop their personal identities amidst many conflicting pressures.' (Richardson and Wood, 1999).

Inclusion is...

 **Building an
Inclusive Ethos** ◀

 Formulating an
Inclusion Policy

 Managing
Inclusion

 Inclusive
Classrooms –
Planning & Teaching

 Inclusive Learning
Environments

 Evaluating
Inclusion

 Further
Information

Building an
Inclusive Ethos

Bringing everyone on board

Inclusiveness is not just about the children. It is about the whole school community. It is easier to include others when you feel included yourself. So this chapter looks at four key factors you might want to consider in managing inclusion inclusively!

- Personal beliefs and vision
- Building learning communities
- Interpreting the context for your school
- Managing the dilemmas

Personal beliefs

'Educators do not jump eagerly out of bed at 6.00am and rush off to school because they wish to raise scores on achievement tests. Engaging in a shared quest to accomplish something special motivates educators.'

(Barth, 1986)

How do I make every child matter?

Since you are reading this book it is safe to assume that you have some interest and beliefs of your own about inclusion. In the last chapter we invited you to develop your own definition. The next step is to create a picture of your ideals for your school or classroom, so ask yourself:

- What sort of a school do I want to see?
- What do I think are the rights and responsibilities of the adults and children?
- What are children going to achieve?
- What sort of personal qualities would I wish for all of them?
- How will people treat each other?
- What is the atmosphere and ethos of the school going to be?
- How will the school work with parents and the community?

Mapping your vision

Mapping your beliefs may be helpful in
organising them to share with other people.

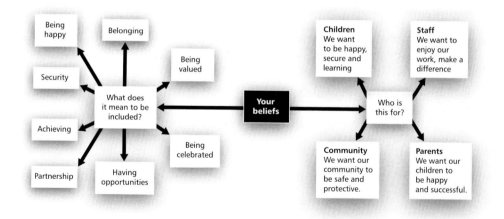

Being
happy

Belonging

Being
valued

Security

What does
it mean to
be
included?

Achieving

Being
celebrated

Partnership

Having
opportunities

**Your
beliefs**

Who is
this for?

Children
We want
to be happy,
secure and
learning

Staff
We want to
enjoy our
work, make a
difference

Community
We want our
community to
be safe and
protective.

Parents
We want our
children to
be happy
and successful.

Creating the vision

The strongest visions are shared ones. So now is the time to start involving other people. An effective way forward is to put together a series of inclusive statements from the perspectives of different groups within the school community. It is up to you who you involve and at what stage but the more people have a say the more people will be backing the school's vision.

The examples opposite show some typical statements.

Creating the vision

Children are included when they:
- Feel that they belong in their school
- Feel good about themselves and their achievements
- Are able to join in with and learn from all classroom activities

Parents and carers are included when they:
- Feel welcome and have positive rapport with staff
- Are treated with respect and have their views taken into account
- Are able to gain access to information and staff

Staff and governors are included when they:
- Feel valued and supported
- Recognise the contribution of their different roles and responsibilities
- Promote effective communication and a positive working environment

Sustaining the vision

Inclusion is a hearts and minds issue. People have strong beliefs and may feel comfortable or very uncomfortable with difference and with change. Respecting individuality and difference and seeing it as an opportunity for richness and creativity is at the core of becoming more inclusive, but with this come challenges to our own understanding and experience of the world and to our sense of 'how things should be'.

How do staff work together to help each other through these challenges and to support change?

Building learning communities

One idea that may be of help is that of the learning community. This is a collegial model of management which enables staff to reflect on and discuss inclusive teaching and learning. What are the main elements of a learning community?

- Shared leadership through staff input into decision-making
- A shared vision based on an 'unswerving commitment' to pupils' learning
- Consistent discussion of how that vision is being put into practice in the work of staff
- Collective learning among staff and application of the learning to solutions that address students' needs
- Peer observation and review of practice
- An ethos of mutual respect and support
- Time and facilities allocated to these activities

(Hord, 1997)

Learning communities in practice

Implementing inclusive practice is difficult. All teachers and teaching assistants
will recognise the feeling of impotence and sometimes anger when you do not know
how to meet the needs of a pupil, or when meeting their need seems to be at a cost
to everyone else. Being part of a learning community means that you are not on your
own. You can tap into the whole school's resources and creative thinking and you can
get helpful feedback when things go wrong.

In one excellent example of this practice a school drew up its list of approaches to
working with children with behavioural needs, exemplified each approach and then
explained why they thought that approach was the right one:

Approach	Example	Why
Express disapproval of the behaviour, never the individual.	*'Stealing is an awful thing to do,'* rather than, *'You are an awful boy for stealing'.*	No one likes to be put down or labelled and where self-esteem and self-confidence are low, such a comment can be harmful and long lasting.

Interpreting the context for your school

There are many internal and external influences that have the potential to encourage, distract from or undermine a school's sense of purpose.

There is a range of tools available to help get to grips with these. The two outlined here can both be used to explore single or multiple issues, at the level of class, department or whole school. Both can be used to explore the perceptions of different groups of people.

The first uses the idea of the continuum. You could develop the basis for your continua from your school's vision statements (page 27) or by using checklists from publications such as the *Index for Inclusion* (Booth and Ainscow, 2002).

Exploring internal influences – the continuum model

When people are responding to a continuum encourage them to think about where the school is at the moment and whether it is moving towards one end or the other or whether the situation is static.

	1 2 3 4 5 6 7 8 9	
All pupils feel they belong in the school.		Many pupils are at odds with the school's values.
All staff can lead school development activities.		Few staff can lead school development activities.
Parents have their views taken into account.		Parents' views are not always welcome.

(Adapted from Ainscow, 1999)

Exploring any unexpected findings or discussing progress on a particular aspect of the continuum provides a mechanism for uncovering and addressing issues.

Exploring external forces – SWOT analysis

The second model, the SWOT analysis, will be familiar to many of you.

Strengths

Weaknesses

Opportunities

Threats

Looking at strengths, weaknesses, opportunities and threats is particularly helpful in identifying external forces which must be attended to and in helping to evaluate the agendas and needs of various interest groups immediately associated with the school. This analysis works well if you carry it out for a number of different contexts and with different groups of people.

Exploring external forces – SWOT analysis

Suppose you are looking at how well you are implementing your race equality policy. You could consider several SWOT analyses looking at the policy in relation to:

- Community links
- The curriculum
- Local and national initiatives
- Staff awareness and training

Or you might carry out a similar exercise focusing on a range of interested groups such as parents, children, local community leaders.

Example SWOT analysis

SWOT analysis: Race equality – the curriculum

Strengths
- We have carried out a curriculum audit
- RE, PHSCE and the arts address a wide range of cultural experiences
- New unit of work on racism
- Contribution of local community groups to the citizenship course

Opportunities
- Work with local history group on the development of our community
- Respond to gaps identified by the audit
- Consider a range of cultural themes when ordering new books and posters
- Include statement on cultural diversity in the curriculum policy

Weaknesses
- Books and images round the school do not represent a range of cultures
- No reference to other cultures' contributions to some subjects
- Work on recognition of the development of the local majority culture is taken for granted

Threats
- Cultural diversity not seen as a priority by all subject leaders
- Limited funding for new resources
- PHSCE co-ordinator leaving

Dilemmas

How do you respect the individuality of a member of staff and a student when that very individuality results in conflict?

How do you ensure a safe and productive learning environment for the majority of pupils, while inclusively addressing the needs of a vulnerable child whose behaviour is challenging and disruptive?

The first stage in managing a dilemma is to recognise it for what it is. Simply knowing that you are trying to reconcile the irreconcilable is helpful. It doesn't stop you persisting, but it places the activity in a context and depersonalises the tensions and frustrations.

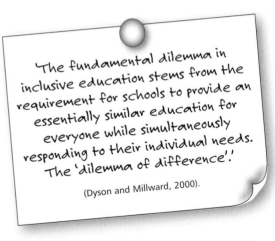

'The fundamental dilemma in inclusive education stems from the requirement for schools to provide an essentially similar education for everyone while simultaneously responding to their individual needs. The 'dilemma of difference'.'

(Dyson and Millward, 2000).

Managing the dilemmas

The next stage is trying to manage and resolve your dilemma. This is likely to involve compromise and the careful management of change. It is at this point that the shared values and vision discussed earlier become a powerful tool in coming to a resolution with little or no conflict.

The idea behind the following model is in three stages:

1. To check your dilemma against your current vision, values and agreed practice.
2. To discuss your findings with someone else who can act as a sounding board.
3. To identify the resources you have available, and make a selection from those resources which will help you to address the dilemma.

When working on stage 3 you might want to involve some other people. Sometimes the available resources seem very small when you are inside the dilemma and alternative/creative ways of using or generating resources refuse to spring to mind. You will know the colleagues and governors who have a positive problem-solving approach and who can support you.

Managing the dilemmas

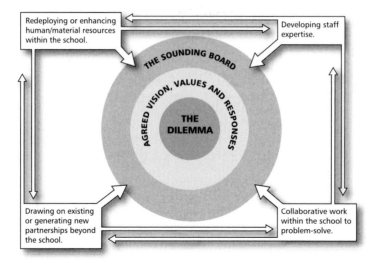

Redeploying or enhancing human/material resources within the school.

Developing staff expertise.

THE SOUNDING BOARD

AGREED VISION, VALUES AND RESPONSES

THE DILEMMA

Drawing on existing or generating new partnerships beyond the school.

Collaborative work within the school to problem-solve.

Inclusion is...

 Building an
Inclusive Ethos

 Formulating an
Inclusion Policy ◀

 Managing
Inclusion

 Inclusive
Classrooms –
Planning & Teaching

 Inclusive Learning
Environments

 Evaluating
Inclusion

 Further
Information

Formulating an Inclusion Policy

The inclusion raft

There are lots of specific policies related to inclusion, some of which are legal requirements. The danger of having so many policies around one area is that they can lose coherence. Having an overarching inclusion policy which describes your school's vision, principles and practice regarding inclusion will help to draw policies for specific groups together and will significantly shorten some of them!

Writing the policy – structure

What sort of content have schools found helpful in an inclusion policy?
It is useful to break down policy into three sections:

- Vision, mission, principles and aims
- Practice
- Monitoring and
  evaluation of impact

Vision and mission

It is helpful here to think about how vision, mission, principles and aims differ. The statements from the activity on page 27 form a very good basis for writing mission, principles and aims as well as describing your vision for inclusion.

The vision is the future picture – how you see your school in 3 and 5 years' time. Mission is how people will see and experience your school now. It is what you are continually striving for. Consider this extract from a school's mission statement:

'...... will be inve....... anything is getting in the way of good progress. taking ...... 'Manorside school recognises the unique contribution of every individual in the school community. It is an inclusive school in which pupils of all abilities and from all cultures and backgrounds are valued and their achievements matter.' This is not to say that all pupils make g........ all the time. M...... .ws th......

- What would you experience when you walked into this school?
- What would the entrance area of the school look like?
- What displays and resources would you expect to see around the school?
- How would students and staff behave towards each other?

Principles

The principles are the core values against which all the activities and actions that take place in the school are measured.

'The good progress of all our pupils is of paramount importance.'

This is not to say that all pupils make good progress all the time. Manorside School knows that that does not always happen. It is saying that this school knows about the progress of every pupil and will be investigating, understanding and taking action if anything is getting in the way of good progress.

That could be:
- Something in the pupil's personal life that they or their family need support with
- Relationships with other pupils
- A teacher's skills in teaching an aspect of a subject or managing a class
- A whole school issue on teaching core learning skills

Whatever it is, Manorside School will be addressing it!

Aims

These are the measurable and observable outcomes of your mission. They guide the priorities that you set in your school improvement plan, and they form the basis of any self-evaluation you carry out.

Taking the principle on the previous page, some of the aims and potential actions have already started to emerge.

The aims could be:

- All pupils will make satisfactory or better progress towards their individual targets

- Parents will be well informed about their child's progress so that we can work in partnership to celebrate success and overcome difficulties

- Any pupils or pupil group experiencing barriers to their learning will be rapidly identified and action taken to overcome each barrier

From vision to practice

Mind mapping is a powerful process in helping to check your practice is linked
to your vision, mission, principles and aims and that you have covered all the angles.

It also helps with one of the pitfalls of working to describe inclusive practice – the
tendency to launch into action-planning and problem-solving, not to mention the
anecdotes! One of the strengths of a mind map is that it allows you to jot down
useful ideas without losing your focus.

So how might a mind map work?

Building a mind map – starting points

We can start with one of the principles and associated aims from Manorside School.

The good progress of all our pupils is of paramount importance

All pupils will make satisfactory or better progress towards their individual targets.

Parents will be well informed about their child's progress so that we can work in partnership to celebrate success and overcome difficulties.

Any pupils or pupil groups experiencing barriers to their learning will be rapidly identified and action taken to overcome each barrier.

Building a mind map – aspects of practice

Using the aspects of practice listed below, and any others you think are important, you can then start to:

- Describe existing practice where this fits well
- Update practice that no longer fits
- Add new practice if you find gaps

Staff responsibilities

Curriculum

Assessment

Parent and pupil partnership

Community

Communication systems

Teaching

Pastoral care

Admissions and transition

Building a mind map – showing the links

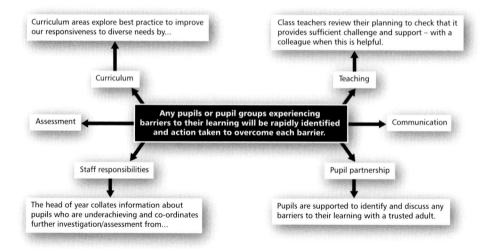

Curriculum areas explore best practice to improve our responsiveness to diverse needs by...

Class teachers review their planning to check that it provides sufficient challenge and support – with a colleague when this is helpful.

Curriculum

Teaching

Assessment

Any pupils or pupil groups experiencing barriers to their learning will be rapidly identified and action taken to overcome each barrier.

Communication

Staff responsibilities

Pupil partnership

The head of year collates information about pupils who are underachieving and co-ordinates further investigation/assessment from...

Pupils are supported to identify and discuss any barriers to their learning with a trusted adult.

Monitoring and evaluation

The words monitoring and evaluation are often linked but the two activities are very different.

Monitoring is about the progress you are making in implementing your plans. Have you written the document, observed those lessons, conducted/provided training?

Evaluation is about the difference that undertaking those things has made on practice within the school and on how pupils are learning.

Inclusive evaluation

Interesting and engaging evaluation processes that encourage everyone to discuss how things are going will help to keep your vision alive.

Effective evaluation:

- Is clear about what is being evaluated
- Is clear about what criteria are being used
- Investigates the impact on pupils' learning and participation
- Involves everyone
- Is on-going
- Celebrates success and identifies priorities for the future

It is worth the effort to discuss and describe how you are going to help each other reflect on and evaluate inclusive practice in your school. Try to achieve a balance that values on-going informal discussion as well as more formal activities or events that draw people's experiences together.

Inclusion is...

 Building an
Inclusive Ethos

 Formulating an
Inclusion Policy

 Managing
Inclusion

 Inclusive
Classrooms –
Planning & Teaching

 Inclusive Learning
Environments

 Evaluating
Inclusion

 Further
Information

Managing
Inclusion

Systems and structures

Much of what we have been discussing is about leading inclusion. This chapter is an exploration of some of the management issues. Thinking back to the teacher in Inclusion Confusion (page 10), how does she know what she is supposed to be doing, whether she has done it and how effective it was?

The staff team

Staff teams in schools are now very diverse encompassing a number of professional, teaching assistant and support roles. In addition to the school's staff, there is an extended team of agencies and support services. As you describe and evaluate your practice in your inclusion policy you will start to uncover strengths and gaps in your staffing. You can use this information to refine your staffing policy and job descriptions and to work out the balance of roles that has the best outcome for different groups of pupils, while making the best use of the resources you have available. A continuum you might want to think about is:

Specialist staff skills ⟹ Generic staff skills

The left of the continuum can be expensive but is reassuring – you know that pupils' needs are being addressed expertly. By training **all** staff you can reduce the air of mystery around specialist skills and ensure that any expensive input is being built upon throughout the curriculum. You are aiming to balance specialism and general awareness of an issue, eg dyslexia or able and talented pupils.

The specialist ⟹ generic continuum

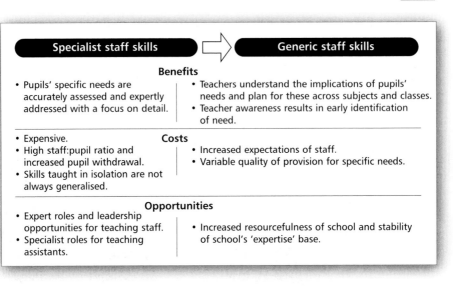

Specialist staff skills ⟹	Generic staff skills
Benefits	
• Pupils' specific needs are accurately assessed and expertly addressed with a focus on detail.	• Teachers understand the implications of pupils' needs and plan for these across subjects and classes. • Teacher awareness results in early identification of need.
Costs	
• Expensive. • High staff:pupil ratio and increased pupil withdrawal. • Skills taught in isolation are not always generalised.	• Increased expectations of staff. • Variable quality of provision for specific needs.
Opportunities	
• Expert roles and leadership opportunities for teaching staff. • Specialist roles for teaching assistants.	• Increased resourcefulness of school and stability of school's 'expertise' base.

Who's responsible?

There are two possible broad structures for leading and managing inclusion:

● Responsibility across the whole of the school's leadership team
● Responsibility lies with one member
  of the school's leadership team

Depending on the size and
context of your school,
middle managers may
also have specific
responsibilities
relating to inclusion.

Both models have
strengths and
potential weaknesses.

Shared leadership and management

Strengths	Weaknesses
Embeds inclusion across all aspects of leadership and management.	Inclusion can slip off the agenda.
Brings contextual expertise (eg knowledge of best practice in curriculum design) to inclusion.	Different line managers, resulting in difficulty creating a cohesive inclusion team in middle management.
Creates manageable roles for schools facing challenging circumstances.	Dependent on good communication systems.
Promotes discussion at a strategic level.	No one has an overview of progress on inclusion policy and strategy development and monitoring.
Brings whole team's strengths and experience into play.	No one has an overview of legislation, guidance and developments.

Individual leadership and management

Strengths	Weaknesses
Advocate for inclusion, keeping it high on the agenda.	Effectiveness is dependent on individual's 'power base' within the school.
Clear line management structures for middle managers with responsibilities for inclusion.	Dependent on individual's communication skills, strengths, expertise and experience.
Individual has overview of inclusive practice in the school.	Strategic decisions may not be fully debated.
High level of expertise in inclusion issues, legislation and guidance.	Difficult to achieve shared ownership of inclusion strategies.
Clear responsibility for policy and strategy development and monitoring.	

Middle management

In developing the practice section of your policy a number of middle management responsibilities will emerge. These may be specialist roles or generic middle management responsibilities. The diagram alongside identifies some of these and shows how job descriptions and policy documents can provide a framework for co-ordinating them.

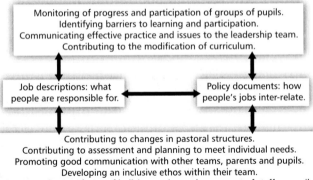

Monitoring of progress and participation of groups of pupils.
Identifying barriers to learning and participation.
Communicating effective practice and issues to the leadership team.
Contributing to the modification of curriculum.

Job descriptions: what people are responsible for.

Policy documents: how people's jobs inter-relate.

Contributing to changes in pastoral structures.
Contributing to assessment and planning to meet individual needs.
Promoting good communication with other teams, parents and pupils.
Developing an inclusive ethos within their team.
Counteracting any forms of bullying, racism or harassment of staff or pupils.

Time to talk

Planning-in time for effective communication to take place pays real dividends.
With open communication in a supportive culture, staff can reflect effectively on their
practice and refine their planning.

Time to talk

It is also important that:

- Line managers understand and are trained to evaluate and feed back on inclusive practice
- Performance management procedures support staff in developing their inclusive practice
- All staff feel included in decision-making processes
- Communication structures for dealing with difficult issues are clear

Inclusion is…

 Building an
Inclusive Ethos

 Formulating an
Inclusion Policy

 Managing
Inclusion

 Inclusive
Classrooms –
Planning & Teaching ◀

 Inclusive Learning
Environments

 Evaluating
Inclusion

 Further
Information

Inclusive
Classrooms –
Planning &
Teaching

The inclusion jigsaw

An inclusive classroom is all-embracing: curriculum, planning, assessment and access strategies are designed to accommodate all pupils unobtrusively.

One way of thinking about this is as a jigsaw with all the elements interlocking to create a picture into which all pupils can fit comfortably. In this chapter we are going to explore learning objectives, teaching activities and access arrangements. In the next chapter we will look at the learning environment.

Doing the jigsaw

You can link the pieces of the jigsaw to the principles of inclusive practice outlined in Curriculum 2000.

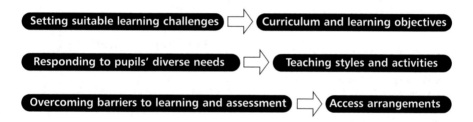

Setting suitable learning challenges ⇨ Curriculum and learning objectives

Responding to pupils' diverse needs ⇨ Teaching styles and activities

Overcoming barriers to learning and assessment ⇨ Access arrangements

Analysing needs

Putting these principles into practice starts with analysing the needs of your pupils. It is helpful to think about needs and your response to them in relation to:

● The characteristics of the whole class – does the curriculum address gaps in learning or is it going over old ground?

● Groups you can identify, eg by ability, literacy or language needs – broad differentiation

● Individuals with specific needs – detailed differentiation incorporating individual education plans

Analysing needs starts with assessment.

Assessment – for teachers

Assessment is a powerful tool in the inclusion toolkit. The combination of formal end-of-teaching-unit assessments, on-going assessment for learning through comments and marking that help you and the pupils know what they need to do next, and moments of reflection with colleagues, parents, or pupils help us to:

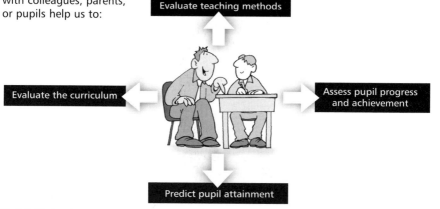

Evaluate teaching methods

Evaluate the curriculum

Assess pupil progress and achievement

Predict pupil attainment

Assessment – for pupils

Tracking progress, clear feedback and the skill of self-assessment help create motivated and independent learners.

Assessment – for parents

Assessment allows parents and school to share a deeper understanding of their child's learning experience . . .

Setting suitable learning challenges

Gather relevant information about your classes including: attainment, progress and needs. You are looking for three groups of pupils: those who may have gaps in their learning, or whose attainments fall significantly behind or significantly exceed the expected level at a particular key stage. Then:

- Identify areas of concern and the class, group and individual starting points in relation to those concerns
- Describe the needs of the group or individual, clearly outlining the starting point and the next steps, eg Group X can talk about their science observations accurately but have difficulty recording these. Aim: to be able to record observations systematically using writing frames to help them structure their work
- Set targets using flexibilities within the national curriculum based on the class, group or individual starting points
- Set up a monitoring system which rewards the pupils' efforts and feeds back into planning
- Refine your learning objectives to address the needs of all groups and individuals

Setting suitable learning challenges

Thinking skills offer a lot of scope for interesting differentiation and add structure to the well-worn phrase 'differentiation by outcome'.

Try working with some colleagues to analyse the potential of a teaching activity for different pupils in terms of the thinking skills shown above. Look for different levels of challenge within and across thinking skills. You could build on this activity by developing a bank of words associated with each thinking skill to use when planning learning objectives.

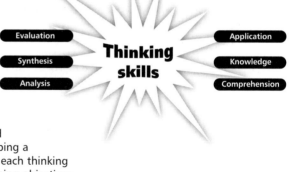

Evaluation

Synthesis

Analysis

Thinking skills

Application

Knowledge

Comprehension

Setting suitable learning challenges

Another way to generate differentiated learning objectives is to use the following concepts:

Broadening – enrichment of the curriculum within class or outside school
Focusing – concentrating on a particular aspect of the objective
Accelerating – where the progression route is clear and pupil has complete mastery
Consolidating – practising skills and concepts in a range of situations
Deepening – involves thinking in a more complex way
Simplifying – reducing the demand on the pupil's independent thinking skills

Start with your core learning objective and then, with different groups of pupils or individuals in mind, consider how you could use these ideas to create the right level of challenge for different pupils.

Responding to pupils' diverse needs

Inclusive teaching is about matching your teaching style and the learning environment you create to ensure that all pupils can achieve. Inclusive teaching:

- Values everyone and provides equality of opportunity
- Creates responsive and effective learning environments
- Secures pupils' motivation and concentration
- Sets challenging and achievable targets
- Identifies supportive strategies which will help the pupils to attain these targets
- Uses a range of assessment approaches
- Removes barriers to learning

Using a range of teaching approaches it is possible to address the learning needs of all pupils, developing their various learning styles, stimulating all pupils to engage and improving achievement.

Responding to pupils' diverse needs

The most effective teaching takes pupils' **learning styles** into account. Pupils learn best within their preferred style but need practice learning in other styles.

 Approximately 40% of school age pupils are **visual learners**. These pupils remember what is seen and respond well to the use of pictures, diagrams, colour coding, highlighting, handouts and practical demonstrations.

 20 – 30% of school age pupils are **auditory learners**. These pupils remember what is heard and respond well to explanations, repetitions, discussion, the use of tapes, poetry, story telling, dialogue, drama and reading aloud.

 30 – 40 % of school age pupils are **kinaesthetic learners**. These pupils remember when they use their hands or whole body to learn, and respond well to practical activities, using three-dimensional models, making things, tactile experiences and moving about.

(Rose, 1995)

The most powerful learning occurs when all 3 learning styles are combined.

Responding to pupils' diverse needs

The range of approaches listed below may well be familiar. The art of inclusive teaching is to think about each activity from the perspective of a group to whom the activity might present a barrier and plan for this. This may lead to you modifying your teaching activity using one of the ideas below or to considering how you provide additional support to enable a pupil to participate. This takes us into the next section on planning for access.

- Using multi-sensory approaches
- Using questioning, explaining and modelling
- Creating structure and predictability
- Balancing didactic and interactive teaching
- Using practical tasks, problem solving and investigation
- Introducing unusual and open-ended learning activities
- Designing a range of independent and collaborative tasks
- Encouraging reflective approaches
- Building in prompts and scaffolding

Planning for access

Access is about making it possible for someone to learn something. More subtly, it is also about pupils feeling that they belong. It is hard to access learning in a place where people like you do not seem to be valued. So it is worth thinking about how images, resources and displays represent the different groups of people in your school.

Thinking about access is not just an individual lesson planning activity. There are benefits in adopting a holistic approach to addressing the learning needs of groups or individuals.

First a bit of encouragement: the better you get at planning for groups the less time you will have to spend on planning for individuals. If you then try to build these approaches into your class planning for the next year you will have anticipated the needs of most pupils. So in the longer term what can seem like a huge workload will diminish – because you know what you have in place and what you intend to do.

What promotes access?

Where pupils are hindered from learning by a physical or behavioural need, eg visually impaired or dyslexic pupils, or those who have problems organising their work or working with others, there are essentially three ways to facilitate access: providing adult or peer support; providing additional materials, equipment or time; or teaching a specific skill before the activity. For example:

- Allowing additional time for completion of tasks
- Using multi-sensory approaches
- Using specific resources including ICT and modified texts
- Using specialist equipment to enable physical access
- Helping students to manage their behaviour
- Supporting pupils with emotional needs such as trauma or bereavement

Good co-ordination is the key here so that all the resources available to school have been identified and all staff know what advice and resources are available.

Managing resources for access

Provision maps are an efficient method of recording what is in place in each class, subject area or year group for all identified groups of pupils. A useful management tool, they support the writing of access plans and strategies, show what you have already achieved, help staff to see what is available and simplify the writing of IEPs. How you construct your maps depends on the nature of your school and the access needs you are trying to address. You can base them on year groups, units of work or pupils' needs – whatever fits.

Year group	Provision/ activities	Monitoring and assessment	Resource allocation
Reception.	Daily speaking and listening programme.	Foundation Stage Profile.	Teaching Assistant 5 hours per week.
	Small group phonological awareness programme.	Developmental checklists.	Teaching Assistant 5 hours per week.
	Structured programme for developing gross motor skills.	Observations by SENCO, teacher and teaching assistant.	Teaching Assistant 5 hours per week.

Provision mapping by identified group

Group and strategy type	Activities	Curriculum		Implications for		
				Environment/ Resources	Staff	Parents
Gifted and talented pupils.	Develop higher order thinking skills.	Questioning in all areas of the curriculum to include opportunities for synthesis, analysis and evaluation.		Resource bank of question types that encourage synthesis, analysis, or evaluation.		

Time to reflect

- Can staff identify and describe the needs of groups/individuals in their class groups?
- Is everyone confident to make decisions about when and how to plan for groups or individuals?
- Am I able to show that action has been taken to meet pupils' needs?

Inclusion is...

 Building an
Inclusive Ethos

 Formulating an
Inclusion Policy

 Managing
Inclusion

 Inclusive
Classrooms –
Planning & Teaching

 Inclusive Learning
Environments ◄

 Evaluating
Inclusion

 Further
Information

Inclusive
Learning
Environments

Creating an inclusive learning environment

The establishment of an inclusive learning environment needs careful planning, and monitoring and evaluation of:

- Routines
- Systems
- Relationships
- Resources

These basic factors influence the day-to-day interaction within the learning environment and are crucial to success within an inclusive classroom.

Classroom management – setting the tone

It is important to develop a pleasant, comfortable atmosphere at the beginning of every day, session and lesson. Have staff reflected on and discussed the following?

Classroom management – setting the scene

Before lessons start it is helpful for all staff to ask themselves some questions.

Are necessary resources available and easily accessible?

Are visual clues available to support instructions and information?

Are materials and tasks differentiated to meet the range of needs within the class or group?

Are symbolic/picture timetables used to give structure to the lesson/day?

Do displays contain supportive and attractive background information that caters for the range of abilities and needs?

Are instructions given clearly and repeated as necessary?

Are different language needs addressed?

Classroom management – expectations

Creating calm classrooms

Have you considered sensitive group dynamics and the concentration level/attention span of pupils when organising your class or group?

Has the working environment been modified to meet the needs of the pupils and the activity?

How can the lesson/activity be modified if pupils lose concentration easily? What strategies can be used?

Is there a plan in place for managing any pupils who have challenging behaviour?

How can distractions be minimised for the whole class and for identified groups?

At the end of the lesson or activity

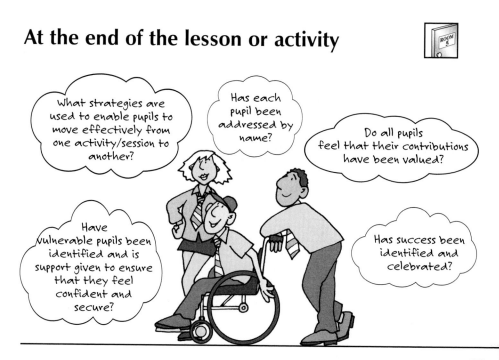

What strategies are used to enable pupils to move effectively from one activity/session to another?

Has each pupil been addressed by name?

Do all pupils feel that their contributions have been valued?

Have vulnerable pupils been identified and is support given to ensure that they feel confident and secure?

Has success been identified and celebrated?

Analysis of systems

The routines we have discussed underpin successful classroom practice and provide boundaries and security for all pupils. Careful monitoring and regular evaluation of routines by staff and pupils will ensure that your school can demonstrate efficient classroom management which meets the needs of all groups of pupils.

Identified problems become points for development. If some of these routines are the source of problems, how can they be changed, developed or adjusted to overcome difficulties? You can develop a range of approaches to meet differing needs and ensure equality of access.

Once successful routines have been established it is important that they are communicated to all staff, adult helpers and pupils so that continuity and consistency of practice can be ensured.

Groupings

Just as effective routines can make a huge difference to pupils' learning and their sense of security in a lesson, so can effective group work. How well is group work used in your school? Are the following groups in evidence in all classrooms across the school?

- The whole class – often used at the beginning of lessons to set the scene, impart new information and give instructions. Also used at the end of lessons to celebrate success, reinforce concepts and knowledge, and share ideas

- Ability groups – usually chosen by attainment. Groups usually work on the same task

- Friendship/co-operative groups – chosen by the pupils or the teacher and usually of mixed ability. Useful for developing co-operative and social skills. Groups work on similar activity or part of the same activity

- Flexible groups – based on needs, strengths, learning styles and preferences and determined by the teacher

Pupils helping each other

The following strategies involve pupils in helping each other to develop social, emotional and co-operative learning skills which will enable them to interact in a positive manner within and outside the school community. Such strategies are effective for group work, paired work, individual work, in lessons and at social times.

In the classroom:

Paired learning

Redrafting

Investigative work

Playing games

Circle time

Editing

Research

Presentations

Shared writing

Pupils helping each other

Breaktimes:

Support strategies such as peer support, buddying and circles of friends extend classroom support into breaktimes for new or vulnerable pupils

Teaching assistants

When planning and implementing an inclusive setting, the role and deployment of teaching assistants is a vital part of ensuring successful practice. Whole school guidance on working together in the classroom can help to establish the sort of practice described in the next few pages across your school. To work together effectively teachers and teaching assistants need time built into their timetables for:

Planning together

Comparing notes

Discussion

Giving feedback to each other

Reflection

Time spent on these activities can save many hours of effort by preventing problems from occurring, or nipping them in the bud.

Teaching assistants – information sharing

Teaching assistants need to:

Have the opportunity to shadow another assistant for a few days.

Understand the rules and routines of the classroom.

Have access to any relevant information about the pupil they are supporting, including individual plans and statements of SEN.

Have the opportunity to exchange jobs within the school/class to develop their skills or provide a better match between the skills of the assistant and the needs of the child.

Know the layout of the classroom and location of resources.

Teamwork – agreeing the systems

In order to provide effective support for all pupils, the teacher and teaching assistant must work together and support each other, give the same message to pupils and follow the agreed systems, particularly:

Entering the classroom.

Asking for help.

Dealing with misbehaviour in the same, consistent way. Agree what behaviours will be dealt with by whom and how.

Responding to and assessing pupils' work.

Being clear about school and class rules.

Teaching methods – approaches to be used in reading, writing, numeracy, etc.

Teamwork – communication

Weekly/daily communication needs to include what is going to happen in each lesson. Teaching assistants need to be clear about which members of staff they should be liaising with.

How much help to give to individual pupils? What special work, if any, is available for the pupils in their care?

Roles and responsibilities – who will do what? Eg:
- Provide individual /small group support?
- Manage the activities of the rest of the class?

These roles can be interchangeable, but careful planning is needed to ensure smooth operation.

Discussing the needs of individual pupils in the teaching group and how they can be met.

Giving feedback:
- Can all pupils cope with the work set?
- Is the work challenging enough?
- Are any pupils unhappy in class or outside?
- Is support being offered where it is needed most and in the most appropriate way?

Reflection

Do the classroom management techniques in place underpin effective inclusive practice?

Are they shared with all staff and do all staff have ownership?

Have children contributed their ideas on classroom rules and routines?

Inclusion is…

 Building an
Inclusive Ethos

 Formulating an
Inclusion Policy

 Managing
Inclusion

 Inclusive
Classrooms –
Planning & Teaching

 Inclusive Learning
Environments

 Evaluating
Inclusion ◀

 Further
Information

Evaluating Inclusion

How do we know if we're inclusive?

Inclusive schools have three key dimensions:

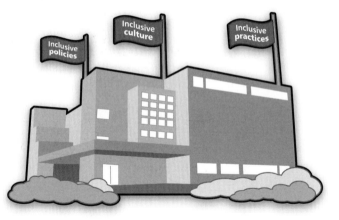

How do we know if they are making a difference?

Evaluating inclusion

What should we be evaluating?

Implementing inclusion policy objectives.

Relationships with parents and the community.

The management and professional development of staff.

Evaluating the impact of strategic plans for inclusion on:

The management of budgets and resources.

Provision mapping, planning assessment and target-setting for individuals and groups with a range of needs.

Pupils' skills, talents participation and progress.

How should we be evaluating?

How well are we doing?
Use a range of quantitative and qualitative data

How do we compare with similar schools?
Analyse data and bench-marking

What is the future profile of needs within our school?
Analyse trends

What does the future hold?
What innovations are in the pipeline, and how will they affect us?

Sources of information

Schools are full of information but some of it is more obvious and easily accessible than the rest. Analysing the performance data for different groups can be very revealing, but that is just the tip of the iceberg.

Inclusive schools are good at looking beyond this to the voices of the people who can explain why the strengths are strengths and what gets in the way of progress.

External test results.
End of module/unit assessment.
Tracking information.
Formative assessment.
Pupil self-assessment.

Monitoring of lessons, planning & pupils' work. Attendance and exclusions data.
Behaviour and reward systems.
Participation/achievements in out of school activities.
Participation in school council, peer mentoring, etc.

The voices of: staff, pupils, parents, governors, partner schools and agencies, the wider school community.

The pupils' views

Ask pupils if they think the school is inclusive.

At lunchtimes there are places where I can go to be comfortable.

I worry about being bullied.

I think the teachers are fair.

It's good to have people from different backgrounds in my class.

Someone is always there to help me if I get stuck with my work.

My family thinks this is a good school.

Sometimes people in my class call me racist names.

I enjoy all my lessons.

Asking parents' opinions

This is valuable in refining and developing practice.

Involving the community

This enables evaluation from a wider perspective.

Some of the pupils came to talk to people at the Over-60's Club, to ask what concerns we have about living in this part of town.

Lots of people from our community work in the school.

The Imam from my mosque is a governor at this school.

There are lots of evening activities at the school, and everyone is made to feel welcome!

After work I coach the school's girls' football team.

One afternoon a week my company lets me go to the school to work as a mentor.

I help teachers at the school prepare letters to parents in my language.

Including the staff

Security, confidence and feeling valued underpins the learning ethos of the school.

Gathering the information

Inclusive schools are learning communities which are constantly reflecting on their own practice.

To ensure that there is consistency across the school, a range of methods may be used to gather information, for example:

- Pupil questionnaires, interviews and self-evaluations
- Parent questionnaires and meetings
- Staff questionnaires and meetings
- Meetings with community groups
- Gathering insights from a 'critical friend'
- Analysing a range of quantitative and qualitative data
- Observation
- School council
- Conversations
- Scrutiny of work and planning
- Ofsted reports
- LA reviews

Analysing the hard data

Attainment and progress data will not tell you everything about how inclusive
a school is but they will show you where the successes and areas for development lie.
They also help you to:

- Demonstrate the progress of every child in every area of the curriculum
- Gain an overall picture of the progress of a child, a group of pupils or
  the whole school
- Focus teaching
- Identify needs
- Inform planning and provision mapping
- Gain an overview of the teaching and learning in the school
- Evaluate the effectiveness of the school's provision
- Demonstrate that you are adding value

Analysing the hard data

Put another way:

What gets measured gets done.

It's easy to apply to a school context the argument that without measuring results you can't differentiate between success and failure:

- If you can't see success you can't reward it
- If you can't reward success you are probably rewarding failure

Further, if you can't see success then how can you learn from it? And if you can't recognise failure how can you correct it?

(See Osborne and Gaebler, 1992)

Who are the vulnerable groups in our school?

It is worth considering who the most vulnerable groups are and therefore where you might concentrate some of your analysis:

- Children who are underachieving
- Children with special educational needs in one or more of the following areas:
  - Communication and interaction
  - Learning and cognition
  - Behaviour, emotional and social development
  - Sensory or physical
- Children learning English as an additional language
- Children from minority ethnic groups
- Very able children
- Children with 'dual exceptionality' – those who are gifted or talented and also have special educational needs
- Children with a disability
- Children in public care
- Children in need

Managing performance information

Facts, observations and voices
All these questions start with hard data analysis but then go on to other evaluative
activities that use observation and listening to different voices to add meaning to the
original analysis.

Questions	Evaluative Activities
Does performance data raise issues about particular groups?	Review planning to check the levels of challenge for able, gifted or talented pupils. Use lesson observations to observe the activities where pupils who are learning to speak English participate well.
Do particular groups of pupils perform better in some subjects than others?	Look at target setting materials to determine if pupils have a greater level of involvement in setting targets and assessing their own progress in better performing subjects. Check pupils' work for evidence of differentiated learning objectives and activities.

Managing performance information

Facts, observations and voices

Questions	Evaluative Activities
Are there more behavioural referrals made from some subjects/teachers?	Use lesson observations to determine the range of learning styles being planned for. Interview pupils regarding the lessons they find most motivating.
Are some groups of pupils absent more fequently than others?	Analyse attendance patterns against particular subjects or times during the week. Carry out return to school interviews with pupils/parents from vulnerable group.
Are there groups of pupils who are under-represented in extra-curricular activities?	Check that school activities do not clash with community activities. Review the menu of activities by discussing them with groups of pupils who are under-represented.

Value added

This is not straightforward. It is not appropriate to think of success just in
relation to national averages. For some pupils small improvements in attainment or
attendance constitute major achievements. You can measure the outcomes of inclusive
practice using a range of quantitative tools, such as:

- Foundation Stage Profile
- National Curriculum levels and SATs results
- 'P' levels
- Standardised tests in reading, writing and maths
- PIPS, MiDYS, YELLIS or CATS
- QCA optional SATs and behaviour scales
- English Language Acquisition scales, such as 'A Language in Common'
- Autumn package

But it is your professional judgement, determined through in-depth discussion about
pupils and analysis of national and local data, that determines targets for individuals
and each identified group of pupils. You can then self-evaluate against those targets.

The outcome

So after all this activity what will you have achieved?

Evidence of children's progress over time.

A clearer vision of teaching and learning in the school.

A clear view of key areas for development - gaps in teaching and learning.

This will lead to further strategic planning and change.

Planning for change

Any significant change within a school's organisation or systems may evoke a range of positive and negative responses from those involved. In an inclusive school change will:

- Value diversity and develop trust
- Encourage the sharing of ideas and concerns
- Enhance the quality of relationships
- Provoke anxiety but enable it to be contained
- Involve all concerned in decision-making processes
- Enable risk-taking to take place without fear of consequences

What next?

Reflection

- What systems are already in place for evaluating inclusive practice?
- Do they supply all the information needed about **all** identified groups?
- If not, what other systems need to be put in place?

Inclusion confusion?

Conclusion

Well, have we cleared the inclusion confusion?

In our experience inclusion can never be an end point. It is a continual process of refining your ideas and attitudes, of testing your practice and trying to understand what that means for the pupils you teach, the colleagues you work with and the wider school community.

We do not pretend to have all the answers, but hope that exploring the ideas and processes outlined here will enable you to build a happily inclusive school.